CATHERINE BERGOI

PORCELAIN PAINTING

The Latest Techniques

ANGO

Copyright © ANGO éditions inc. 1998
4519, rue Saint Denis
Montréal QC H2J 2L4 - Canada

General Editor: Gérard & Josiane Boulanger
Photos: Jacques Vigouroux, Peter Maidment
Layout: ANGO éditions
Filmsetting: ANGO éditions
English adaptation: Jonh Tittensor

Printed by Colorcraft, China

ISBN 1 894 185 03 X

Contents

Pansies
Catherine Bergoin, 1996.

Foreword

Monic Montu
Winner of the 1986 French Government Award for Excellence in Porcelain Painting.

When Art Becomes a Passion

Porcelain painting as a profession calls for real dedication. You have to be absolutely meticulous and determined to see the job through to the end, even when a single piece requires many hours' work.

As you can imagine, preparing the design is a highly detailed, delicate business - and then there are the various firings along the way. But before that you've had to choose the piece to decorate and find the right design for its shape and size. Painting the design then becomes a real labor of love. When I was young my ambition was to find a profession in the artistic domain, one that would give the greatest possible scope to my love of drawing. Little did I imagine that one day I would be taking classes in porcelain decoration - and that thanks to my teacher I would end up catching a virus I've never regretted!

And so a few years later I found myself transformed into a fully fledged craftsperson, working professionally in an area that makes its own specific demands. Painting flowers, birds, landscapes and so on according to your inspiration is simple enough, but the results have to please your public - and give you the urge to further improve your designs, your color work and so on. And when this happens - you're hooked!

In 1986 I had the good fortune

Catherine Bergoin

The author was born in the Savoy region of France in 1949. She began her working life as a physical education teacher, but like the other members of her family she spent a lot of time exploring the different paint media - oils, watercolor and so on - on every imaginable kind of surface.

Then by chance, one day in 1980, she stumbled on the technique of porcelain painting. In search of the answers to her many questions about this fascinating discovery, she studied with countless painters, not only in France, but also in Germany, Switzerland, Italy and Finland.

The meeting with Monic Montu was crucial. Armed with what she had learnt from her new teacher, Catherine Bergoin returned to her native Savoy and transformed her favorite pastime into a full-time job.

to take out a French Government award for porcelain painting; for this my painting had to come up to the most exacting expert standards, which meant a lot of hard work indeed.

It was just at this time that I was giving classes in porcelain decoration. Some of my students were extremely gifted, but there was one I remember in particular because of the speed with which she picked up the technique. Her name was Catherine Bergoin: she had the simple, enviable knack of being able to draw well and come up with the right color schemes, and with each day that passed her painting skills increased. For her art is a true passion and she has the gift of knowing how to share her enthusiasm with others.

Monic Montu

1. *What you need*

Paints, brushes and assorted equipment

Watercolor brushes
- Isabey series 6227
- Raphael series 8404
- Leonard series 297 RO

For laying the colors, you'll need brushes of different sizes and different types, such as red sable and maybe squirrel hair.

Stipplers
- Raphael series 16331, for getting good even coverage.

Fan brushes
- Raphael series 8274, for laying down backgrounds.

Cut liners, slanted end
- Raphael series 16434, for accurate line work.

"Clean-up brush"
- small, fine, for dipping in pure alcohol or methylated spirit.

Spatulas
- for mixing your paint powder with the medium. Be careful not to buy them too flexible, or you won't be able to mix properly. The aim is a smooth, non-granular mix with the same consistency as toothpaste.

A glazed bathroom tile
- to use as a palette. This is better than a sheet of glass, which should be used solely for mixing your colors. Choose a white as close as possible to porcelain white; that way you'll have a good idea of what each color will look like on the surface of the piece you're working on.

Pillboxes
- for storing your paints once you've mixed them. Note that plastic containers are advised against for storing paints in powder or mixed form.

Pencil: Stabilo Schwan 8008
- for drawing on the porcelain. This is a greasy graphite pencil that leaves no trace after firing.

An HB pencil and a fine ballpoint
- for transferring the design from the tracing paper on to the porcelain.

Tracing paper, graphite paper
- for transferring the design.

Scotch tape
- for holding the tracing paper securely in place on the porcelain.

A selection of brushes.
Top: fan brush.
From left to right : 2 stipplers, "clean-up brush", squirrel hair, cut liner.

Masking fluid
- use red for preference. For more detailed information, see chapter 10.

Different types and sizes of pen
Copperplate nib, for upstrokes and downstrokes.
Italic nib, for fine lines.
Mapping pen for the really fine details.

Paints
- bought in powder form

Liquid products
Universal medium for mixing the paints.
Spike oil or lavender essence, for diluting paint prepared in paste form (modern technique).
Turpentine, for diluting paint prepared in paste form (traditional technique).
Citrus essence, for cleaning your equipment.
Pure alcohol or methylated spirits, for pushing back colors.

Articles to paint
- pieces made of porcelain, earthenware or stoneware.

Pillboxes for prepared colors; dropper for spike oil; spatulas; foam sticks.

Nylon foam sticks
- these are synthetic foam cylinders in diameters going from 4 to 40 mm (approx. 0.15" - 1.5"). They can be used instead of a stippling brush when there are large areas to cover.
They're easy to clean: methylated spirits or warm soapy water will do the trick. Let them dry in a dust-free place, then store them in a closed container away from daylight and ultraviolet light.

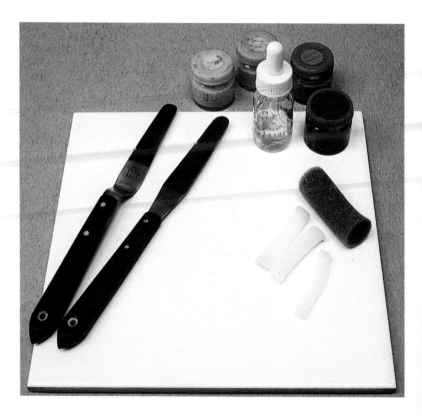

Different pens for different strokes…

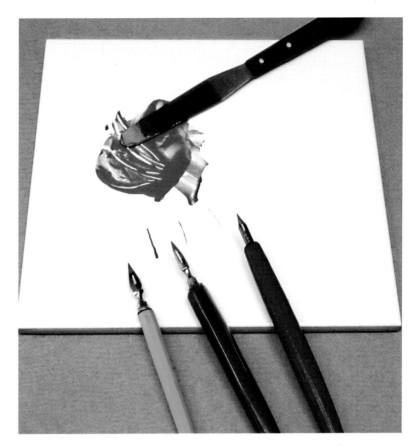

Odds and ends
- for transporting pieces once you've painted them, you'll need something that closes firmly: a Tupperware container or other plastic box is ideal.

Typical decoration pieces.

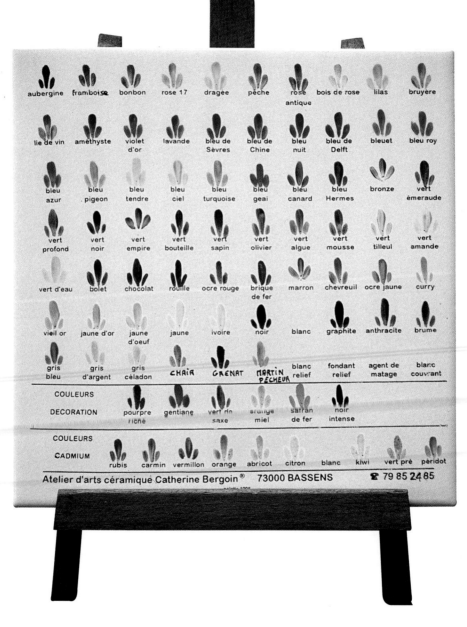

The palette
You must have a chart showing the colors after firing.

2. *Painting :*
before, during and after

Mixing your color paste

For this vital operation, I advise you to use a white glazed tile rather than a plate or a square of glass. This is because the shape of the plate makes mixing difficult and the glass, being transparent, doesn't let you see the color as exactly as you need to.
Place a little powder on your tile, add some universal medium and mix the two together with a spatula. (NB: The grains of powder are clearly visible at first.) Mixing time can vary according to the brand of powder, some being more granular than others. The end result after five to ten minutes' work should be a homogenous mix.

The best method is to mix small doses one after the other until you've got a sticky substance just slightly thinner than toothpaste. Store your prepared paint in a pillbox. Put a label on the pillbox to indicate the color - and another one on the lid, so as to avoid unforeseen mixtures of colors.

Suggestion
It's preferable not to mix all your powder at once, since after two years or so the paste becomes unusable. The powder, on the other hand, lasts indefinitely.

After adding the medium, you have to work with the spatula until you get a good, even mix.

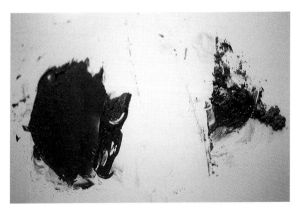

As it dries out inside the pillbox, the paste breaks up into compact little balls. When you want to re-use the color, put the pillbox (if it's made of glass) in the oven at 120°C (250° F) for an hour. Take it out of the oven, let it cool and then grind the paste up; you can now use the powder as before, without any loss of color.

Preparing and using the paints

Freshly made up (and for some time after), the paste is easy to handle. To prepare the paint, take several little dabs of paste, put them on your white tile and mix with a drop of spike oil.

Spike oil is in fact lavender essence in a less refined state, and you can use either here. Another possibility is natural essence of cloves. The main difference between the two - apart from the odour! - is that clove essence evaporates more slowly.
Increasing the dose of spike oil means you can put the paint on with a pen, but first mix with the spatula until the paint is good and smooth.
As you work, remix regularly with the spatula and add a drop of spike oil from time to time - it evaporates fast!

> **Color chart**
> Since the colors can change considerably during firing, a chart showing the fired colors is essential.

A word to the wise

If the color is too oily
- firing can produce bubbles and spatter the paint over the surface of the piece.

If the color is put on too thick
- it will flake off during the firing, taking the porcelain glaze with it and leaving a "hole" in your design.

If the layer of color is too thin
- the color may come out dull and opaque. If this happens, you have to put on a new layer of color or flux (see p. 73), then re-fire.

Make sure you remove all hairs and dust from the paint
- if not they'll show up after firing. Always bear in mind that firing really makes any defect more obvious.

You can always darken fired colors, but it's too late to lighten them.

Porcelain pieces can be fired many times: the famous Sèvres bleu, for example, takes ten firings.
With each firing, the piece in question actually becomes harder and more robust.
By contrast, earthenware reacts badly to multiple firings. Three should be taken as a maximum.

Finishing touches

When you've finished decorating a piece, put your paint - as long as you've managed to keep it clean - back in its pillbox. You can use it again later. The great thing about our method, as opposed to various others, is that there's practically no waste of paint.

Cleaning your equipment

When everything else is out of the way, it's time to set to and clean your equipment, with either citrus essence or methylated spirit.

Citrus essence has the advantage of an agreable odour and, being oily, it keeps the hairs of your brushes in good shape.

Personally, I prefer citrus essence: as a cleanser it's quick, efficient - and it smells good.

Transporting finished works

Immediately after firing the painted design is very fragile and pieces need adequate protection if you have to take them from one place to another.

In most cases a rigid plastic food container will do the job.

Memo board *Catherine Bergoin 1995*
(For the blackberries, see Chapter 5).

3. *Hints on Stippling*

So what exactly is stippling?

Stippling - one of the basic techniques of contemporary porcelain painting - involves pressing the colour on to the surface with an up-and-down movement of a brush called, logically enough, a 'stippler'. The aim is to avoid visible brush-strokes and thick layers of paint which might flake off during firing. The size of the stippler will depend on the surface to be covered. The larger the brush, the more even the coating; but a big brush makes detailed work impossible, which means you need stipplers of different sizes. When the surface involved is really extensive - a background, for example - we generally use foam sticks instead of a brush.

Stippling with a brush, using a repeated up-and-down movement. Here the left hand side has been stippled.

Stippling with a foam stick. The action is the same as for the brush.

*For this project we're going
to decorate a plate for
a young child.*

Preparing the porcelain

First of all wash the piece, then
carefully remove all traces of
grease, using a clean rag and
methylated spirit (or pure
alcohol) or turpentine, as
appropriate:
- *traditional technique:* turps or
methylated spirit
- *stippling technique:* turps or
methylated spirit
- *relief white:* methylated spirit

If you're using a Stabilo 8008
pencil for your drawing, you'll
get a clearer mark if you clean
with turpentine.

The drawing

It's best to begin by choosing a
simple design for your first
efforts, since first of all you
have to reproduce it on the
piece.
Take a look at the back of your
plate: the trade mark points to
the top and your design should
take account of this - but if
there are mounting holes in the
back, they should naturally go
at the top. So mark the top of
the working surface with a
cross, using your Stabilo 8008.
You can place your drawing
either directly, with the Stabilo

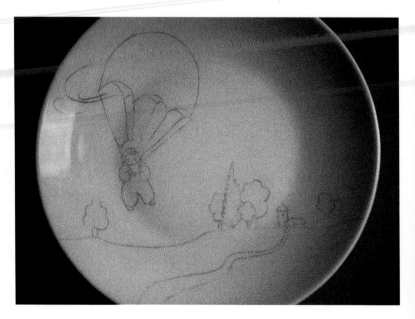

*The initial drawing, done with a
Stabilo 8008 pencil.*

16

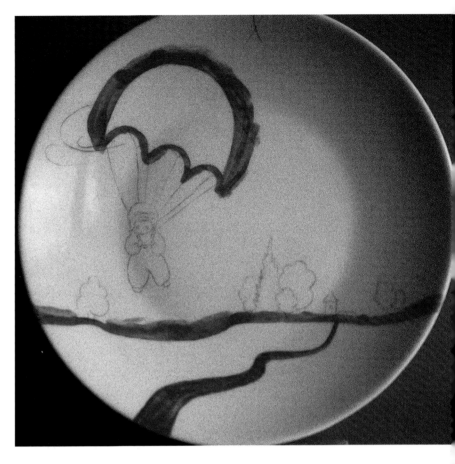

(the mark disappears during firing) or by using graphite paper or tracing paper.

If you use tracing paper, start by copying the design on to it with an HB pencil. Turn the paper over and retrace the drawing on the back with the Stabilo.
Then place the paper on the porcelain with the Stabilo tracing against the surface and fix securely with adhesive tape, so that the drawing can't move. Now take a ballpoint and carefully trace over the drawing, which will thus be transferred on to the porcelain. Take care not to leave out any part of the drawing; a trick that will help here is to have oblique lighting on your work table, since this will give a shiny line along the parts of the drawing already traced over with the ballpoint.

Masking around the areas to be painted

The first step is to use masking fluid to mark out the major areas to be painted, this is important, because these areas will be worked with a foam stick and not with a stippler. Using the foam stick also has the advantage of letting you work fast and cover a large area before any of the paint dries. This gives a much more uniform result than working with a brush.
At the same time, the sticks are much less precise; so to protect the details along the edges of these areas, a line of masking fluid is essential. You should use the red fluid (it's the easiest to see) and lay down a good thick coat; if it comes out a pale color, it's too thin and you should add a second coat, otherwise the fluid will be hard to lift off.
Note that this product removes pencil marks, so avoid painting it over your drawing.

A little tip
Masking fluid quickly spells death to brushes - so use your old brushes for putting it on and as soon as you've finished, clean them with solvent.
The Raphael 8204 brush is perfect for this part of the job.

The parachute

For the parachute I use sky blue, white and blue-gray. Since the area to cover is quite large, I opt for a Raphael 8274.6 fan brush.
To get the color gradation right I use sky blue lightened with white, then pure sky blue next to it, then sky blue darkened with blue-gray.
In this way I cover the entire surface, working quickly but carefully and overlapping the masking fluid very slightly. Once the paint is on and before it dries, I begin stippling the parachute area with a foam stick around 2 cm (3,4 in.) in diameter.
Note that I always start with the lightest color and finish with the darkest. Logical, but easy to forget.
Next, I get rid of the masking fluid, lifting it off with a toothpick or a small pair of tweezers (for further details see Chapter 7, "The Apple").
I carefully check that no trace of masking fluid remains on the surface and that the paint hasn't "crossed the line".
For the underside of the parachute I use blue-gray, stippled with a no. 8 brush. Then I dilute the blue-gray with spike oil so as to be able to draw the parachute strings with a pen.

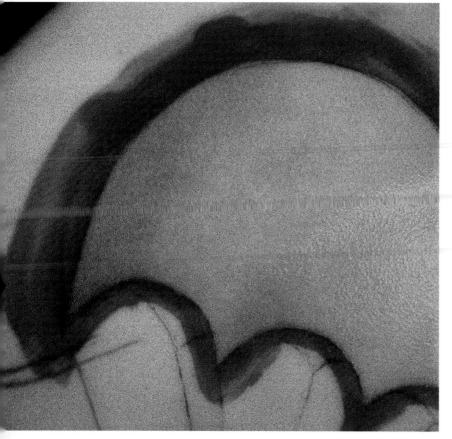

The parachute is stippled with a foam stick.

*When the parachute is finished,
I move on to the figure.*

The figure

Each of the colors used here should be applied with a squirrel hair brush of a size that suits the area involved. I stipple, then I tidy up the outer edges with my "clean-up brush", dipped in pure alcohol or methylated spirit.

The "clean-up brush"
You use it for tidying the edges of painted areas - and for nothing else! This brush has to stay absolutely clean and must not contain any trace of paint. Since pure alcohol or methylated spirit repels the paint, I use them on this brush to get one hundred per cent clean edges.
After dipping the brush, I wipe the head down with a cloth to get rid of the excess spirit, then trace around the edges of my color area to get them nice and precise.
Note that here you have to work towards the color: the spirit doesn't take paint off, it just dilutes it, so it's vital not to draw the paint out on to the porcelain: if you do, the traces, however faint, will show up after firing.
It's equally important not to

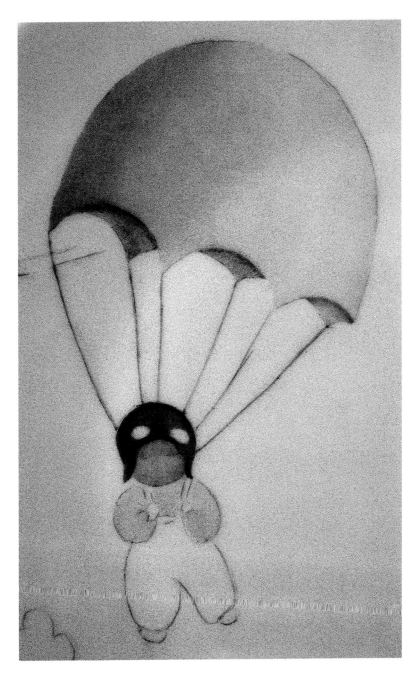

have too much spirit on the brush, or your color will dilute; so wipe down with the cloth before starting.

The colors
You can get the child's skin color right using the flesh tint (see the color chart, page 10).

This gold-based color takes on a pink tinge during firing, so I take care to lay down a very fine coat: otherwise the final result will come up too strong. I stipple with a no. 6 stippler, then paint in the fringe with old gold, running a fine line of color over the flesh tint of the face.

19

Above:
The land area is stippled with a foam stick.

Bellow:
The land area is finished, so I remove the masking fluid. Note that the fluid also removes the pencil marks.

The pullover is painted with sea-green, the helmet and trousers with azure, the goggles, the parachute straps and the shoes with Delft blue. The order of painting the colors on owes nothing to chance: the pullover goes into the trousers, the goggles go over the head and the parachute straps go over the pullover.

I also work from the top of the picture to the bottom: this means there's no risk of contact between my hand and the fresh paint.

The ground area

I fill in this area with a Raphael fan brush 8274.6, using a mixture of yellow and lime for the upper part, pure lime for the middle and last of all moss green for the bottom.
I then stipple with a foam stick 14 or 20 mm (0.5-0.75 ins) in diameter, working (of course) from the lightest color to the darkest.
After taking off the masking fluid I check for mistakes. If there are corrections to be made, I make them quickly, before the paint has dried.

The trees

Here I use the same greens as for the ground area, but adding in some emerald and dark green for variety and visual accuracy.
For a clump of trees, I begin with the one furthest away and work towards the nearest one. If it happens that two adjoining colors mix, then your paint is too liquid: when the consistency is right the colors don't mingle on the painting surface.

Details

The facade of the church is sea-green and the roof blue-gray.
The upper part of the little road is lilac, then I bring in a mix of mist and lilac for the middle. The lower part of the road is done with mist.

In the interests of overall harmony, I re-use the lime/yellow land mix for the trees. Touches of blue-green create a visual link with the figure.

For clearer definition, I let the paint dry, then outline the light areas with a fine brush.

Once the paint is dry, I tidy up the details and outline the light-colored parts of the design - the child's pullover, his face, the parachute - with blue-gray. For this, I use a 297.0 brush, which gives a very fine line. Doing this when the earlier paint is dry prevents any mix with the main color.

Laying down the fine line means not having to paint over an existing coat: this latter always carries the risk of creating a thick layer of paint that might flake off during firing.

At all times I keep a close eye on the overall harmony of the composition and the color-scheme.

The memo board *(see also p. 14) shows a beautiful balance between the piece and the design.*

The name

After diluting the azure with spike oil, I write the child's name with a pen.

The consistency of the paint is vital here: if it's too liquid the color will quickly begin to spread and thin out. Remember that the paint is much thicker than ink and flows much more slowly towards the point of the nib. This means you have to write slowly and at a regular pace so as to get a clear, uniform line. The surface of the porcelain wears the pens out rapidly and you'll find you have to change them often.

21

The finished piece. After firing all trace of the pencil drawing has disappeared.

Observations

The colors mentioned above (and elsewhere) are just suggestions. You can try out any color scheme you like, as long as it's harmonious overall.

Don't put the paint on in thick layers: you should always be able to make out the white of the porcelain through the paint. To get really dark colors you need two coats, with a firing between them.

Give added realism and variety to your designs by using different amounts of paint in different areas.

Last but not least, don't forget to give your brushes a thorough cleaning between colors. And as long as you use a Stabilo 8008 pencil (or a graphite tracing), the initial drawing will disappear without trace in the course of firing.

Handy hint

If you're in a hurry you can gain time by drying a coat of paint with a hairdrier.

4. *The sugar technique*

Why sugar?

The advantage of this technique is that in a single operation you can lay down the design and fill in the areas to be painted, then fire.
The standard color mix - powder, universal medium and spike oil (or lavender essence) - does not dissolve the sugar drawing.
This means that you also cut down the number of firings.
The sugar technique is often used for designs done in outline form, such as characters from a comic strip. As a rule the work is done with a pen, but you need to remember that this gives a thicker line than the powder/medium/spike oil mix. The sugar mix dries very fast and you need to keep adding drops of water - which means you have to be careful not to ruin the consistency of the mix. The best idea is to limit this technique to purely decorative items, since the mix does not hold particularly well on the porcelain.

Oval dish with orchids
Catherine Bergoin - 1995.

Preparing the mix: 3 parts paint powder, 1 part sugar.

The mix

Any kind of sugar will do the trick here, but icing sugar is handy in that it dissolves faster than the others.

My personal method is to mix icing sugar and paint powder in the following proportions:

**3 parts paint powder
+ 1 part icing sugar**

Then I add a few drops of water until I get a creamy substance liquid enough to be applied with a pen.

Mixing hints

- *Too much water* will give a light color that will take a very long time to dry.

- *Too little water* means you won't be able to draw, since the mix won't flow down the nib.

- *Too much sugar* will give a thick, very raised line that will be slow to dry. The end result will be a fragile design likely to break up after firing.

All the colours from the palette can be used and you can mix them if you want to increase your range and use different shades.

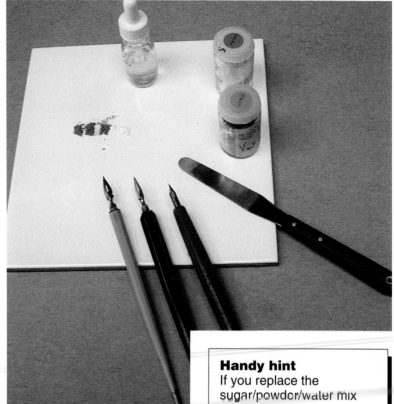

The water evaporates as you work and so you have to keep on adding more.

You also have to clean your nib with water from time to time, to stop it from filling up with dried mix. Water is used for all cleaning operations involving the sugar/powder mix.

Handy hint
If you replace the sugar/powder/water mix with water-based medium/powder/water you'll get the same result. The latter mix has the advantage of dissolving the powder better, being more fluid and flowing better along the nib. We should note in passing that American porcelain painters replace the sugar and water with Coca-Cola; while the Germans, not to be outdone on the patriotism front, prefer schnapps.

Right:
The design is outlined with a pen.

Below:
The first colors are painted on and stippled. The powder/medium/spike oil mix in no way damages the sugar outline.

A plate

After first cleaning the porcelain thoroughly, I lay down the drawing, working either freehand, with tracing paper or graphite paper.
I then prepare my sugar mix, using graphite gray - black is too dark for this kind of design. When the drawing is completely redone with the gray sugar mix, I wait until it's perfectly dry.

Now for the bottom part of the picture. Always remember to start at the top, so as to avoid any contact between your working hand and the fresh paint.

Then I start putting down the colors, using the usual mix of powder, universal medium and spike oil.

I put the paint on in the normal way; there's no need to worry about the areas done in sugar, as the two products don't mingle with each other at all.

I can cover the sleeve or the pocket of the dress with peach; since the color is transparent the sugar-mix lines of graphite gray will show through without any problems.

THE COLORS USED

THE LITTLE GIRL'S DRESS	*peach*
THE LITTLE GIRL'S FACE	*flesh tint*
HER HAIR	*yellow ochre or red ochre*
THE STORK	*roebuck*
THE FIR-TREES	*bottle green*
THE MOUNTAIN	*bottle green, rosewood*
THE FIRST BUSH	*curry, yellow ochre*
THE SECOND BUSH	*chestnut, rosewood, antique pink*
THE FIELD IN FRONT OF THE MOUNTAIN	*bottle green, rosewood, roebuck*
THE FIELD IN FRONT OF THE HOUSE	*yellow ochre, roebuck*
FOREGROUND FIELD WITH ROAD	*peach, rosewood, antique pink*
FOREGROUND FIELD WITHOUT ROAD	*roebuck, rosewood, lime*
THE HOUSE	*roebuck*
THE ROOF OF THE HOUSE	*yellow ocher, red ocher*

The plate, finished and fired. You'll notice that the colors - especially the pinks - come out brighter after firing.

The Grape Jug, *Catherine Bergoin - 1996*

5. *Advanced stippling*

A TART PLATE

Getting the volume and the details right

Since this is a painting exercise, I chose my design according to the possibilities it offered for simplifying and stylizing.

Using tracing paper, I transfer my drawing on to the porcelain, eliminating any details that are too finicky or unclear. I have to be particularly careful with the leaves: this part of the design has to be absolutely true to life, which makes it much harder to get right than the branches or the grapes.

Once this stage is finished, I have to decide where the light is coming from and indicate this with a big fat arrow drawn in pencil.
This arrow is my guide to defining the various lit and shaded parts of the design. Putting the arrow right there on the porcelain makes it hard to forget this very important consideration.
When I choose the lighting angle, I have to remember that oblique lighting coming from the right or the left is going to create much more interesting effects than any form of direct lighting, which always has a tendency to flatten the image.

The vine branch

As a general rule, branches are cylindrical.
To get the illusion of volume across, I use at least three colors or three shades of the same color.

For our design we're going to use:

- for the light color (the lit area)
Old gold

- for the medium color (the main one)
Roebuck

- for the dark color (the shadow)
Chocolate

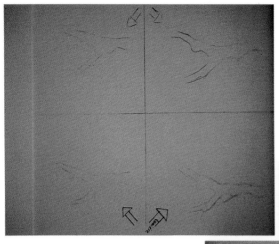

Branches, with a choice of lighting.

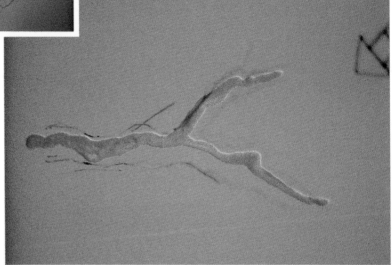

Step 1a: Putting on the light color.

Step 1b: Putting on the medium color.

Step 2: Putting on the dark color.

Step 3: Stippling, followed by outlining of the edges with the clean-up brush.

To ensure good color harmony, I now modify these colors:
- to the chocolate and the old gold I add a tiny quantity of roebuck.
I do the same to the roebuck with the two other colors, and so on. It's not a question of changing their character, but rather of altering their "key" by slipping in a reminder of the other colors. This involves proceding by very small quantities, touching in a little bit at a time and being careful not to end up with the same color three times over. Sometimes it's interesting to try out a monochrome design (see also Chapter 6). You could take, for example, China blue, cornflower and pigeon blue: as it's a matter of three different blues, you don't have prepare the mixes mentioned above.

Where do I start?

If you always work from light to dark when painting and stippling, you save yourself the trouble of having to clean your brush with each change of color.

"In nature, branches can be any color at all - or just about."

Ivoire
Chevreuil
Bolet

gris vert céladon
chevreuil
vert bouteille

Bois de rose
Framboise
Chocolat

Bleu pigeon
Bleuet
Bleu de Chine

Laying in the colors

The order for putting down the colors is from light to dark. Here the lightest color represents the lit part of the subject.

I put it in the upper quarter of my branch because, as the direction of the arrow shows, this is where the light falls. For esthetic reasons, get into the habit of laying in your colors as indicated in the photos on pages 30 and 31.

Step 1
I begin with the highlight, using the lightest color.
Then I move on to the medium color, which is the main one for the branch. I place wide, irregular strips of color on the lower part of the branch and narrow (but still irregular) strips on its upper part.

Step 2
Still without having to rinse my brush out, I paint the dark color (the shadow) on to the lowest part of the branch. Using the same color, I then outline the top outside part of the branch.

Step 3
I take a stippler of the same diameter as the branch - in this case a number 8 - and I do the stippling in one go, moving the brush steadily along the branch.
The stippling has to be done uniformly, so as to blend the colors into one another and avoid having to go back over the design.

Step 4
I take my "clean-up brush", dip it in alcohol or methylated spirit and redraw the contours of the branch to get a good clean edge. The aim here is not a straight line, but one that is faithful to the vine branch: a bumpy, irregular line, in other words.

NB: In nature, branches can be any color at all - or just about. Above are a few examples, all using the light color, medium color, dark color system. Take note of the different lightings used and the different effects they create.

32

Not just a blotch, but a real piece of fruit

To paint the individual grapes we're going to use the following colors:
- raspberry
- golden violet
- Sèvres blue

You'll note that I always get visual harmony via three colors: a light, a medium and a dark. Here I can add in grapes using a single color, or two colors, or all three.
In nature just about anything goes in terms of shapes and colors, but here we have to get the shape and layout of the fruit just right. I should mention that for reasons of clarity and easy understanding, this bunch of grapes has been simplified.
When, with a little practise, you can paint it just right, you'll have the pleasure of being able to move on to more complex subjects, such as the Grape Jug (see p. 28).

A little logic goes a long way.
Next, and taking care to avoid any contact with the branches (since they haven't been fired

I work grape by grape, finishing each one completely before moving on to the next.

Note the shades of color created when two grapes touch.

33

yet), I start painting the fruit, working from the center out. Why? Try working in the opposite direction and you'll get the message!

Before beginning, remind yourself that no grape is perfectly round; and that a bunch of grapes is not a bag of marbles.

This means varying your shapes, but without losing touch with reality - after all, Mother Nature has never come up with grapes in the form of cubes.

Putting on the paint

As I work on the grapes I bear in mind that I need to put more paint on the shadow areas, since I'll soon be stippling them - and this takes paint off.

The closer I get to the lit part of the grape, the thinner the coat of paint. By the time I get to the top quarter of the grape, I'm putting on just a thin veil of color.

I work over the grape with a number 10 stippler, then use my clean-up brush to lay bare the white of the porcelain: this gives me the highlight.

This white area has to have the same curve as the grape and must also be in proportion to its size.

In nature or in your imagination, grapes can be just about any color.

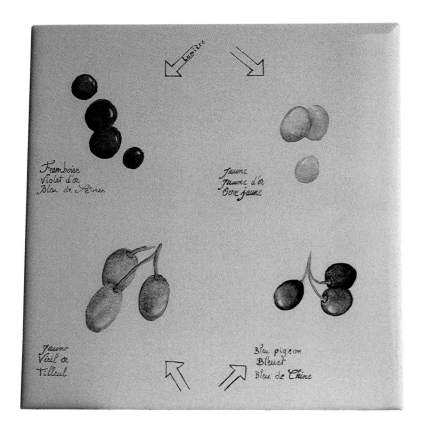

So make sure that your highlight is not just a white patch, but an area that imitates the overall shape of the grape.

When two grapes are in contact with each other, I either paint each in a different color or use varying intensities of the same color. The aim here is to prevent the two shapes from coming together in a single mass.

The parts of the grapes that are touching will be painted darker, because of their curve and the fact that each throws a shadow on the other.

The lower of two grapes will also be darker, since it falls in the shadow of the higher one.

In nature a bunch of grapes is a compact whole. Ours is going to have one side lit and the other side in shadow; this means that the individual grapes in the shadow area will have more or less the same color density, but without being completely uniform. In addition, this density will decrease as you move closer to the lit area.

After stippling the grapes with a number 8 stippler, if necessary I go round the grapes with the clean-up brush to give them a clear outline.

Using my judgement, I can also change my stippler according to the size of the grape I'm working on.

A few tips

• For this kind of work I never clean my brush: the resulting color mixes give me a range of shades that are more subtle than the colors I started out with.

• Remember to vary the colors of your individual grapes as you go along, but without using a system. Above all, don't make the mistake of making one part of a bunch all the same color and its neighbors all a different color.

• When two grapes are touching, always begin with the darker one. You'll find that it's much easier to lay down a light color beside a dark one than vice-versa.

35

Below:
Starting to put the colors on: you begin with the lightest.

Bottom:
Stippling: always remember to work from light to dark

Opposite, above:
I draw in the veins, then use the clean-up brush for the serrated edges.

Opposite, below:
Close-up of another leaf, showing its underside. Note the difference in color between the two sides: the underside of a leaf is often lighter.

Leaves: a network of veins and colours

Even for small leaves I always prepare plenty of different colors on the white tile I use as a palette.
Seeing the colors together this way allows me to imagine the kind of effects I can get on the finished leaves.

For this project, let's try the following colors:
- lime green
- moss green, forest green
- golden yellow
- old gold
- curry

I just love autumn leaves: they offer a great range of colors and sometimes some really unexpected ones.
When necessary I also make myself an extra green by mixing moss green and Sèvres blue.

I find it preferable to darken colors by adding (for example) a dark blue rather than black. Black irretrievably deadens other colors, leaving them cold and sad-looking.
In the interests of color harmony, I opted here for Sèvres blue as a darkener, since it already figures elsewhere in the design.

The overall color scheme has been harmonized and now the plate is ready for firing.

Laying down the colors

I begin with the light colors, painting them carefully but irregularly along the edges of the leaf. As the work on the leaf goes ahead, I move gradually into the dark colors - but at no time do I clean my brush! All these colors, whether light or dark, need to be put on thickly, since the stippling takes off a substantial amount of paint.

When you stipple this kind of leaf it's most important to work from the light colors towards the dark ones - and here too, remember not to clean your brush.

I opt for a number 10 stippler, since the area involved is quite large.

When the stippling is completed, I take a number 2 pointed brush and dip it ever so slightly in the moss green - just enough to make the hairs of the point stick together. Then, while the paint on the leaf is still wet, I draw in the veins.

A word of warning

A vine leaf has no midrib. If you look closely you'll see that in fact there are five veins of equal size, branching out from the stem. For a start, then, stay with the distinctive look of the vine leaf. Later on you can invent and improvise to your heart's content.

You'll also need to bring in some secondary veins branching out from the main ones. These will naturally require a finer line.

Drawing a fine line
Note that the more you hold the brush vertically, the finer the line it gives. Take care not to overload your design: the aim should be overall harmony rather than a perfect imitation of what nature offers.

The plate after firing. You'll note the changes in the colors, especially the violets and purples.

Getting the serrated edges right is a bit more complicated and calls for a steady hand and a precise touch.

As usual, this part of the job is done with the clean-up brush: dip it in pure alcohol or methylated spirit, then wipe it with a cloth before starting.

And don't forget:

For tidying up the contour of the leaf, you should start at the stem and work your way towards the point. I work holding my clean-up brush parallel to the edge of the leaf: this is the standard way of using this brush. When I want to create a point on the edge, I run the head of the brush backwards and slantwise into the leaf itself. The backwards motion should last only a millimeter or two (0.1 in.), then the brush should move off forwards again.

As soon as the clean-up brush starts to fill up with paint, I clean it; this ensures that it will keep on doing its job of defining the serration by creating a clean outline.

If you're not too sure of yourself here - I mean, if your brushwork is a bit unsteady - practice a little on your white tile before starting on your edges.

39

Right, above:
The initial color is applied in the same way as for the grapes (see p. 33).

Right, middle:
With my number 1 stippler I work berry by berry, starting with the lightest side. The arrow indicates where the light is coming from.

The **Raisin Jug** (see p. 28) was painted in the same way, using the following colors:
Branches: chestnut, yellow ochre, ivory
Leaves and fruit: yellow, lime green, fir green, dark green, yellow ocher, red ocher.

Blackberries and raspberries

Blackberries and raspberries (pages 40, 41) are painted in the same way as the grapes, using Sèvres blue for the blackberries and aubergine for the raspberries.
In your initial drawing it's enough to outline the overall shape of each berry, without putting in all the little bumps.

The **Memo Board** (see p. 14) was done using the same technique and with the following colors:
Stems: wild mushroom, fir green, turquoise
Leaves: bottle green, fir green, emerald, turquoise
Fruit: Sèvres blue
Flowers: white, sky blue, silver gray, mist
Centre of the flowers: golden yellow, wild mushroom
Stamens: golden yellow, curry.

Below:
As I work, the stippler picks up more and more paint, so the "bumps" on the berry become darker and darker. When I've finished the berry, I make room for the sepals by pushing the color back with the clean-up brush.

Top:
I put in the stems and sepals, then add the color for a small, unripe berry.

Above:
I stipple, put in the sepals on the little berry and repeat the operation for the other berries.

Top and bottom right:
Raspberry Jam Pot, with detail.

Blackberry Butter Dish
Catherine Bergoin, 1996.

6. *Monochrome designs*

Sometimes what suits a particular piece or decorative style best is a single-color pattern or design. The choice of shades can still be very varied: for example, you can start with a medium color then change it at will by lightening or darkening. Let's take the examples shown below.

Shading your colors

The first idea that comes to most beginners' minds is that you darken a color with black and lighten it with white. White in fact doesn't pose too many problems, although certain precautions have to be

	Medium color	Light color	Dark color
BLUE	azure	azure + light blue	azure + china blue
PURPLE	antique pink	antique pink + pale candy	antique pink + chocolate
GREEN	moss green	moss green + almond green	moss green + dark green

Hazelnuts in close-up.

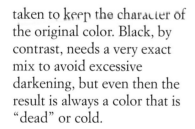

taken to keep the character of the original color. Black, by contrast, needs a very exact mix to avoid excessive darkening, but even then the result is always a color that is "dead" or cold.

Used in the right place at the right time, a cold color can really add something, but an entire composition done in this way tends to come out lifeless and disagreeable.

This means you need to watch your mixes carefully - and remember that the color you see on your mixing tile can easily change during firing. For this design, I start out with three different blues:

- cornflower
- pigeon blue
- turquoise

The cornflower is the darkest color and will be used for the shadows on the branches, the fruit and the flowers.
The pigeon blue is the medium color and the turquoise, being the palest one, will allow us to

44

A handsome wild rose. *A dogwood design.*

light the design.

You're already familiar with the way of working:
- clean the porcelain
- do the drawing, either freehand, with tracing paper or with graphite paper
- lay down the palest color, the one that brings in the light (here it's turquoise)

- lay down the intermediate color (pigeon blue)
- lay down the dark color (cornflower).

Once the colors are in place, you stipple the design with a stippler or a foam stick of the appropriate size.

You finish by using the clean-

up brush to get the edges of the branches and the fruit perfectly outlined.

Note that when a creator signs a piece on the back or the underside of the base, it's usual to opt for a color that figures in the design.

Anemone Vase
Catherine Bergoin - 1995.

7. A choice of fruit

An apple

Once I've got the drawing down on the porcelain, I outline it with masking fluid. For this design I'm going to use the following colors:
- yellow, golden yellow
- old gold
- raspberry
- peach

Painting and stippling

For the paintwork I use a Leonard 297.8 brush, starting with the lightest color and working through to the darkest.
I pay attention to the quantity of paint, since the stippling will take off quite a lot. I stipple with a 14 mm (half-inch) diameter foam stick to get a fine-grained look.

First off, I lay down the masking fluid; this means I can stipple faster, using a foam stick. As soon as the fluid is dry, I paint on the colors: yellow, golden yellow, old gold, peach and last of all, raspberry.

Stippling done with a foam stick
Don't forget to lighten one area so as to show where the skin of the peach catches the light.

As usual, I stipple from light to dark without pausing to clean the foam stick. This kind of work calls for practise, since you need a sure hand so as to avoid having to go back over the painted area. You also have to finish stippling each color before moving on to the next one.

A few tips
Don't forget to put some light on the piece of fruit and to make this area match the overall proportions of the apple.

A peach, on the other hand, is fuzzy and non-reflective: this means that the light will have to be shown, not by using the porcelain surface (as for the apple), but with a very thin layer of paint which, after

firing, will give a very pale tint. You'll need to thoroughly blur the edges of this highlight area, so as to make the matt skin of the peach show up well.

Next, I take off the masking fluid, making sure no fragments stay stuck to the surface.
Now it's time for the first firing, after which I put in the shadows before firing again.

I paint the stem with wild mushroom, fir green and roebuck, then the leaves with yellow, bronze, fir green, dark green and peach.

The apple is now ready for the first firing.

For maximum precision I prefer to put the shadows in after the first firing - using in this case very liquid wild mushroom. Then I fire again, with the results you see here.

The peach:
golden yellow, yellow ocher, raspberry, peach.
The leaves: lime green, yellow ochre, seaweed and a mix of lime green/red ocher.

The peach

For smooth, shiny pieces of fruit, I bring in the highlight by using my clean-up brush to take the color off, right back to the white of the porcelain.
A peach, however, has a fuzzy skin; to get the highlight I have to reduce the thickness of the color, but without going all the way back to the white.
As the stem - painted in wild mushroom, fir green and roebuck - crosses the body of the peach, I mark it in first with masking fluid. I later take this fluid off along with the strip around the outside of the peach.

After the first firing, I put in the shadows using very dilute chocolate and raspberry. Then I fire again.

8. *Flowers*

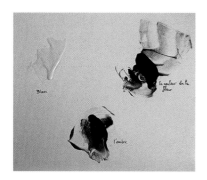

The wild rose calls for three base colors: white, antique pink, blue-gray.

For the petals, I create different shades of pink by adding varying quantities of antique pink to the white.

To get the shadow colors, I add blue-gray to each shade of pink.

Wild roses

The wild rose is pale pink all over, but things are more complicated than they first appear: to give this design life and solidity I need, in fact, to use several different colors.

I start with antique pink and lighten it with white in such a way as to get three variants of the original color.

I then divide each of the three variants in half and to one half of each I add a little blue-gray; in this way I obtain my shadow colors.

With the antique pink as my starting point, I now have six tints, each with the same color base; this allows me to paint all the different parts of the wild rose, whether they are lit or in shadow.

Note that if you paint your shadow using gray only, you will end up with a gray patch on your flower that will not provide the effect you're looking for.

The petals

First of all I paint the branches and the leaves, which will be partly covered by the flowers. Next, I take each flower petal by petal.

Before starting a new petal I always finish the preceding one. I begin with the lower petals, using the pale pinks; then, without cleaning my brush, I move on to the darker colors.

Once I've laid down all the colors for a petal, I go over the whole area with a number 8

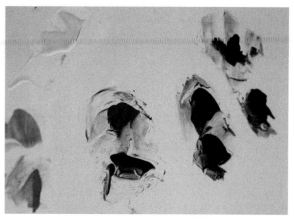

The branches and the leaves are painted first, with fir green, seaweed, lime green and antique pink. Then I start the first petal.

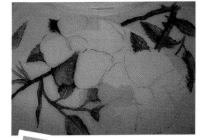

The petals, in order: first of all I paint those that are underneath. I stipple each petal as I finish it, then tidy the edges with my clean-up brush.

The corolla is finished.
If the paint is still wet, I make room for the heart using the clean-up brush; if it has dried the heart area will have to be scratched off with a toothpick.

I paint the heart: golden yellow, yellow ocher, chocolate. For esthetic reasons the heart is oval rather than round.

stippler, working from the pale colors through to the dark ones.

As the heart of the flower is to be painted last, I deliberately paint over its edges a little; this means I can scratch the paint off with a toothpick so as to get the exact shape of the heart.

Lastly, I finish the edge of the petal with the clean-up brush.

Handy hint
When one petal partially obscures another, the underneath one should be shadowed in the contact zone and the upper one painted in a pale color.

This difference in color will give you a clear separation between the two petals.

Curled leaves

If a petal is curled back in such a way as to show both its upper and lower sides, the lower side should be painted darker, since it's in shadow.

So either I don't paint this part and I mask out the curved area, or I push the paint back with my clean-up brush and replace it with a darker color that I then work over with a number 2 stippler.

I finish the outer edge of the curve with the clean-up brush. Since the upper side of the petal is in the light, I need to take a paler color than that used for the underside or the curve.

On certain flowers you'll note that the underside is a quite different color than the upper side.

However there's no problem with wild roses, since both sides of the petal are the same color. But take care, the light will be different.

Don't forget, either, that a curled petal has a quite different shape than a "flat" one.

The heart

When all the petals of a flower are finished, I open up the heart by scratching off the excess paint with a toothpick. Then I take a good overall look at the design so as to get the heart/petal/stem relationship right.

Here I need two colors: golden yellow and yellow ocher.

I paint the major part of the heart with golden yellow, outline the shaded edge with yellow ocher and stipple with a number 2 brush. To finish the heart of my wild rose, I place a patch of lime green in the center and blur its edges with the same stippler.

For the stamens, I choose at least three colors, in this case golden yellow, yellow ocher and chocolate. Then I place specks of color all around the heart, with no attempt at uniformity where placing, size and shape are concerned.

I use the golden yellow for the lit side of the heart, moving gradually towards the chocolate for the shadow side. I put in few lines to indicate the stalks of the stamens - but a lot less than in reality, to avoid visual confusion.

Wild rose sauceboat
Catherine Bergoin - 1996.

The stamens are added after the first firing.

Bowl with violets
Catherine Bergoin - 1996.

The bowl with violets
The petals: golden violet, heather, lilac.
The heart: curry.
The leaves: lime green, seaweed, dark green.

I begin with the underneath petals, stippling them with a foam stick. The right-hand petal has not yet been stippled.

The pansy
- *The petals:* peacock blue, jay blue, turquoise.
- *The dark part of the petals:* China blue, Sèvres blue.

Pansy Breakfast Setting
Catherine Bergoin - 1996.

White flowers: the christmas rose (or "hellebore")

I started out by painting the stem and the leaves, using a mix of lime green, old gold and white to get the pale green I wanted. The darker green is in fact bottle green and for the roses I used antique pink and rosewood. The procedure is more or less the same as for the vine leaf (see Chapter 5).

• The white flowers will be painted with - white!

• For that lighter shadow, use lime green and silver gray.

• For the darker shadow, use bottle green; you could maybe add some antique pink.

Painting and stippling

I begin by painting the petal in white, using a Leonard 297.5 brush.
Next in order comes the lighter shadow, followed by the darker one: these colors are always painted directly over the white.

The edge of the petal is initially defined by the pencilled outline, but after firing this line will no longer be there; so I redraw it, using a very fine Leonard 297.2 brush and starting with the lighter shadow color.
I then alternate the light and dark shadow colors so as to avoid making this line too regular. Last of all, I stipple the whole area of the petal, working as usual from light to dark. I don't clean my stippler as I go, and I pay close

attention to the edges of the petal, which should integrate well into the whole.

For the following petal, I work in exactly the same way, going particularly carefully for the part in contact with the previous one.
Here, the light-colored paint should slightly push back the darker color of the first petal, so as to provide clear definition of both and put even more emphasis on the shadow.
For the petals that have a

curve, I follow my usual system, beginning with the underside and finishing it completely before starting on the curved part.
As it happens, the color of the curve is different, which makes my job that much easier. I use antique pink and rosewood.

To bring the work to a close, I stipple the edge of the petal then add the finishing touch by redefining the edge with the clean-up brush.
The outer edges of the curved part will be shaded with a mixture of bottle green and antique pink, which will give me a good strong shadow.

As for the stamens: they have to be painted in yellow, across the white of the petals. To get this part right I scratch off some white with a toothpick: this way I avoid getting a buildup of paint that could all too easily start to peel off after firing.

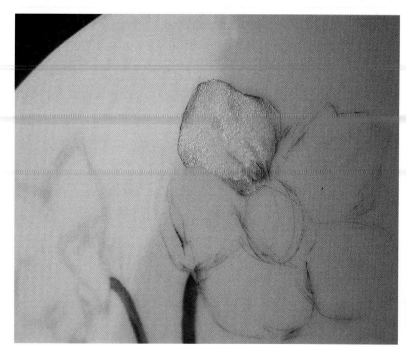

The petals are finished. I outline the shape of the heart and bring in the curves with antique pink.

I finish the flowers with a heart made up entirely of stamens in old gold, yellow ocher and wild mushroom.

The Cherry Pot
Catherine Bergoin - 1995.

9. Reds and cadmium colors

Way back when...

If you used reds and oranges in the "good old days", you had to be sure to take it into account at firing time, as they often had to be fired at 750° C (1380° F).

For working on earthenware this presented no problem at all , but on porcelain you had to finish all the other colors, fire at 800 ° C (1470° F), then add the red and orange and fire again - at the lower temperature, naturally.

But now...

Almost all the colors available on the European market are manufactured by a single company in Germany and are fired at the the same temperature, including the cadmium reds and oranges.

Minimum firing temperature is 850° C (1560° F). However, there are certain limitations in regard to these reds and oranges, which can be mixed together only in certain cases and not at all with non-cadmium colors.

This means no gradations of colors. You can only put on the color as it comes out of the container, which means having to have a lot of different paints.

Here are a few examples of the unfortunate results you'll get after firing if you try to mix your cadmium reds or oranges with normal porcelain paints:

mix	watercolor	porcelain
red + yellow =	orange	*yellowish*
red + white =	pink	*grayish*
red + blue =	violet	*blackish*
red + black =	red	*dark, unattractive*

Cadmium colors

The names of the colors in this group always include the mention "cadmium".

Real reds, real oranges

These are the only colors that allow you to get real reds and real oranges.

There are ten of them in all:

- cadmium ruby
- cadmium carmine
- cadmium vermilion
- cadmium orange
- cadmium apricot
- cadmium lemon
- cadmium white
- cadmium kiwi
- cadmium field green
- cadmium peridot.

Firing temperatures

To fire cadmium colors, use one of the programs below, according to the piece you're working on:

Earthernware
normal cycle, 760° C (1400° F)

Porcelain
2 - 10 hour cycle,
850° C (1562° F)
30 - 90 min. cycle, 850°-920° C
(1560°-1688° F)

N.B. To make cadmium colors work, you often need three firings at different painting stages (see further on in this chapter).

Cadmium colors on their own

Considerable care is needed here: these colors change greatly during firing, so an accurate color chart is more vital than ever.
To be sure of getting good bright colors, you need two coats of paint, with a firing between the two.

• *Ruby, carmine, vermilion, orange, apricot and lemon can all be used together in any proportion you like.*

Example
- A first coat of vermilion.
- Then a firing.
- If the result is satisfactory, I then add a second coat of vermilion to get a really bright finish.
- However if the fired color is too red, I paint on a coat of apricot or lemon to yellow it somewhat.
- If the fired coat is not red enough, I add a coat of ruby or carmine.

• *Ruby, carmine, vermilion, orange, apricot and lemon can all touch the cadmium greens (kiwi, field, peridot) and cadmium white without causing any problems.*

• *Ruby, carmine, vermilion, orange, apricot and lemon can all be used with cadmium peridot in any proportions.*

The pear: moving from cadmium red to a normal color.

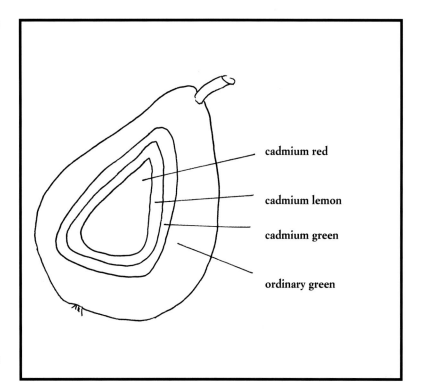

cadmium red

cadmium lemon

cadmium green

ordinary green

Cadmium and standard colors

Cadmium lemon and cadmium greens
These colors can touch the other colors of the standard palette or be mixed with them in any proportions without loss of brightness or other undesirable effects.

Mixing does not necessarily give the desired result
• After firing, cadmium lemon + yellow ocher give an almost identical yellow ocher.
• The same applies for cadmium lemon + red ocher.
• Before firing, cadmium lemon + royal blue give a green which turns blue during firing.
• Cadmium field green + dark green give an almost identical dark green after firing.

It's worth noting that the colours obtained by mixing cadmium yellows and greens with colors from the standard palette are always the same after firing.
The results can be quite interesting, so why not try firing a palette of test mixtures?

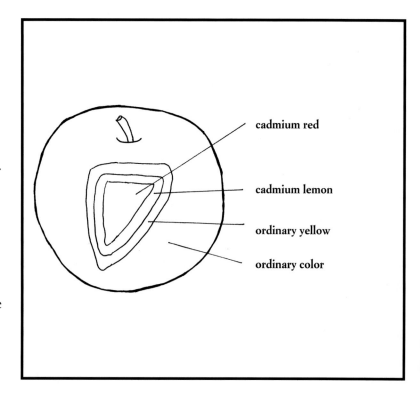

The apple: moving from cadmium red to a normal color.

cadmium red

cadmium lemon

ordinary yellow

ordinary color

Cadmium lemon and greens have their equivalents in the normal palette:

Cadmium lemon: yellow.

Cadmium kiwi: lime green.

Cadmium field green: moss green.

This characteristic allows us to mix these colors: for example, we can paint a spot of cadmium ruby on a piece of fruit or a leaf, then outline it with cadmium lemon, continue on with yellow and then bring in other colors from the normal palette.
The same process can be followed for a cadmium green and a normal green.

Cadmium ruby, carmine, vermilion, orange and apricot
These colors do not mix with colors from the normal palette. Mixing cadmium ruby and ordinary white intially gives a pink, but after firing this becomes a grayish marbled color.
Mixing cadmium orange and yellow gives an orangey yellow, but after firing the result is the same marbled gray.

It's important to be aware that these color changes are irreversible and that all you can do is throw the piece away. Even when cadmium reds and oranges have been fired, any normal color that comes into contact with them will produce the same dismal gray marblings.
This result will recur with each firing, to a more or less marked degree according to the colors that come into contact with each other.

66

A group of cherries: *the stalks are painted with cadmium field green, and the cherries themselves with cadmium carmine and cadmium apricot.*

Handy hint
To lighten a cadmium color, you can add:
- 20% cadmium white to: ruby, carmine, vermilion
- 30% cadmium white to: orange, apricot
- 50% cadmium white to: lemon, kiwi, field green, peridot

Note that if you go beyond these proportions your colors will turn irremediably gray.

First firing: *I make the black line as fine as possible, then paint the cherries with cadmium ruby. I add the highlight, then I fire.*

Second firing: *Since the color has been absorbed by the surface of the porcelain, I paint on a second coat of ruby to get a good bright tint. I paint the leaf with a non-cadmium green, then fire.*

Third firing: *Using very dilute black, I shade the cherries (to give them the necessary volume) and the part of the leaf touching the black line (to conceal the line). Then I fire.*

Opposite page
Jam jar
The redcurrants were painted in the same way as the cherries on this page, using cadmium vermilion.
Before the third firing, I shaded the berries with very dilute black and added a black spot for the shrivelled flower. The stems are painted with cadmium kiwi.

68

Cadmium ruby,
cadmium carmine

Same color
+ yellow dots

Black

Cadmium carmine,
cadmium lemon, cadmium kiwi

Same color
+ yellow and bottle green dots

Black

Getting smart

How to move from a cadmium red or orange to a color belonging to the normal porcelain palette:

- If you want a gradation from cadmium red or orange to yellow or green, use the technique shown in the drawing of the pear (p. 66).

- If your aim is a direct changeover from a cadmium red or orange to a color from the normal palette, you need to leave a tiny space between the two zones.

- Cadmium red and orange do not react with black, so you can use a fine line of black to separate them from any normal color.

A word of warning
All brushes, stipplers and foam sticks used for cadmium colors must be perfectly clean, for the slightest trace of any normal color will irreversibly change cadmium red or orange into a disagreeable shade of gray.

To guard against this eventuality, some of my students have brushes, stipplers and foam sticks that they use exclusively for the cadmium colors. They mark them in a distinctive way so as not to confuse them with their regular equipment.

Strawberries
From left to right: the evolution of two strawberries. The higher one is the riper of the two.

Opposite:
Strawberry Breakfast Setting
Catherine Bergoin - 1996.

10. *Useful additives*

Opposite:
Candy box with gold band
Catherine Bergoin - 1996.

*This candy box required two firings,
the first being for the flowers and the
leaves. After covering these with
masking fluid, I added the background
color, stippled it and fired again.
Flowers: raspberry, white.
Leaves: chocolate, roebuck, white.
Background: wild mushroom, roebuck,
white with flux added.*

Flux

Although there's already a
certain amount of flux in every
color, you can also buy it on its
own.
Its function is to create shine
by making the paint penetrate
the glaze.
There are many different kinds
of flux, which are fired at the
same temperature as the
paints.

All-purpose flux
When you're working, you can
add flux to your
paint to
increase the shine of the design.
Generally speaking, very pale
designs or pastel-colored
backgrounds tend to emerge
from the firing with a matt finish.
If this is not the kind of result
you're after, you can take
remedial measures by covering
the design with a fairly liquid
coat of flux, stippling with a
foam stick, then re-firing.
To avoid this second firing,
you can add flux to the paints
to be used for the design or the
background.
The flux is prepared with
universal medium. You can
store it in a pillbox and dilute
as necessary with spike oil.
As a rule the mix is one part
flux two parts paint, but with
experience you'll find that
other mixes are possible
according to the effect you're
looking for.

Never mix flux with cadmium
red or orange or paint it over
these colors. The results will
invariably be disagreeable -
and irreversible.

Protective flux
As the name indicates, this
product protects designs on
porcelain. You paint it on after
the final firing, to make your

Limoges blue vase: the fuchsias were painted on using a mix of relief white and relief flux, then fired at 820° C (1500 F).

work more resistant - less vulnerable in the dishwasher, for example. It also reduces those annoying squeaks produced by knives and forks.

Relief flux

This product is added to relief white, as a way of stopping the latter from crackling during firing.

Masking fluid

This is a plastic varnish which is used either to mask areas to be painted later, or to protect already-fired parts of a design. Easy to apply in liquid form, it can be peeled off like a rubbery film when no longer needed.

Several kinds of masking fluid are available:

Colorless

This type is rarely used now, since it is difficult to see when the time comes to remove it.

Blue

Widely used in silk-screening, it is less common in porcelain painting for more or less the same reason as the colorless variety.

Pink (the most widely used)

This type stands up particularly well to the presence of medium, spike oil, fat oil and turpentine in the paint. Its edges stay perfectly clear.

It is used for masking off areas around which paint is to be applied.

It should be applied thickly, so as to produce an intense pink color which makes removal easy. If an application gives only a pale pink color, let the product dry and add a second coat. According to the thickness of the coat, it takes between one and two minutes to dry.

Once the fluid has dried, you can paint on the necessary colors and stipple without any problems.

When your paint is thoroughly dry, carefully lift the dried fluid with a toothpick or tweezers. It will peel off like a rubber skin. When using this product, don't forget to clean your brush immediately afterwards, using the special solvent. If the masking fluid dries on the brush, all you can do is throw the brush away.

For the same reason it's best to use an old brush for this part of the work: the bristles don't stand up to the ravages of the

---

Masking fluid
Always check that all the product has been removed: otherwise it will run during firing and leave traces on the porcelain.

---

fluid for very long.

You must absolutely not speed up the drying of the fluid by any means whatsoever: the mask will become brittle and very difficult to remove.

Water-based masking fluid

Used in the same way as the preceding product.

Relief white and relief flux

These products allow the porcelain painter to imitate the relief whites used in certain Asian techniques, to accentuate the edges or the curls of petals or to get the most out of a highlight.

Begin with a mixture of 50% relief white and 50% relief flux. This is the standard mix, but with a little experience you'll learn to vary it.

The two products are to be

---

mixed with water-based medium, then diluted with water until you get a paste that should be thicker than your usual paints.

The maximum relief you can get on porcelain is 0.5 mm (0.02 ins).

Relief white

This product is always used in conjunction with relief flux, which stops it from crackling in the kiln. It's possible to vary the proportions:

- *more relief white than flux* gives a more opaque color;
- *more relief flux than relief white* gives a more translucent color.

Relief flux

Can be applied alone over a finished design to get a sort of translucent relief effect, but the relief will be milky in color.

Colored relief effects

Relief products can be colored at the preparation stage by the addition of a maximum of 3% paint. This way you can create markedly pastel colors without any loss of solidity. Note however, that brick red and the cadmium colors cannot be used for coloring reliefs.

An alternative technique is to lay in the relief without coloring it, then fire before adding gold or the desired color (excluding brick red and cadmium colors).

Unfortunately the results here are unpredictable: it's easy to end up with bubbles or a tarnished surface.

To get good results every time you need to have really mastered the art of firing.

White-out

Porcelain colors being transparent, there's no way of using them to create a white motif on a colored surface.

This product is slightly opaque and used in the right way allows us to overcome this problem.

Sometimes it takes two coats, with a firing between them, to get a convincing white.

This product is used in the same way as normal colors and can be mixed with them.

Matting agent

This is a white powder that is added to the paint in proportions from 20% to 50% and which enables us to create satin or matt finish colors.

You prepare it in the same way as paint, with medium and spike oil.

At the next stage, mix the paint and matting agent thoroughly, but without letting the latter go beyond 50%.

Note that this product whitens the colors very slightly.

To get good visual impact, you can contrast neighboring areas of very glossy color (made with flux) and matt areas (using matting agent).

This product meets European safety standards for use in the manufacture of plates, etc.

Citrus oil

This is an essence with a most agreeable odour and can usefully replace turpentine and methylated spirit at brush-cleaning time.

In addition, its slight oiliness helps keeps the bristles in good condition.

As it dries it hardens a little and makes the bristles stick together, so you should stroke the head of the brush into the right shape before putting it away.

When you want to use the brush again, you will need to dip it in citrus oil so as to separate the bristles.

For allergy sufferers, this is the best alternative to turpentine.

Oil of cloves

This essence, noted for its strong odour, is widely used in various branches of porcelain painting.

It is used, among other things, to facilitate writing on porcelain with a pen and tracing fines lines with a brush.

You can slow the drying of your paints - and thus gain extra working time - by adding a few drops of oil of cloves to your paints.

A word of warning however: it makes masking fluid soften and become extremely difficult to remove.

Another use for water-based medium: take the paint powder/water-based medium mix, dilute well with water and use the result to get convincing "watercolor" effects.

Water-based medium

Both the standard medium and mixing oil contain around 25% turpentine, which denies allergy sufferers the pleasure of painting on porcelain.
Water-based medium, on the other hand, is turpentine-free and can be recommended without restriction.
You begin by mixing it with paint powder until you get a paste slightly more fluid than toothpaste, then you dilute with water according to the the way you intend to work.
All cleaning can be done with water.
If you like, you can draw your designs using water-based medium in place of the sugar technique described in chapter 4.

Metallic colors

This type of paint powder actually contains different metals. Metallic colors can be mixed with each other.
Their preparation is the same as for normal paints, but the paint is more granular.
You fire them at 850° C (1562° F).

11. *Firing tips*

Firing

Short cycle
Firing time: maximum 2 hours
Final temperature: 950° c (1740° F).

Firing time: the time taken to get from room temperature to the final temperature.
Final temperature: temperature at the end of firing.

N.B. If your colors show up matt after firing, or if the pinks come out carrot-colored or the purples turn greenish, then the kiln has not reached the necessary final temperature. The answer is to fire again, but increasing the temperature setting by 30° C (85° F).

At 850° C (1560° F)

Your colors will come out beautifully glossy and well embedded in the porcelain glaze. Most importantly of all, if you've bought approved paint powder, your pieces will not constitute a health hazard.

At 950° C (1740° F)

Fired at this temperature, your purples and blues will take on extra depth and warmth. Note that the cadmium colors stand up to this temperature without any problems.

Paints and standards

Before being used, the basic products used for the manufacturing of porcelain paints are ground and mixed for hours by a machine that can handle up to a ton of material at a time.
After this initial grinding, the mix undergoes what is called gravity-sifting: it passes through a powerful jet of air and the smallest, lightest particles are separated out from the heavy one.
The large, heavy particles are then returned to the mixer to be ground up again.
The powder is then burned under intense heat in a kiln; the temperature in the kiln can go as high as 1400° C (2550 ° F), at which point the powder liquefies.
The liquid is then drained off from the kiln, into an enormous vat of cold water.

The sudden drop in temperature transforms the liquid into a dull-colored crystalline material which looks something like glass. This material is dried, then fed into a rotary crusher containing thousands of steel marbles. After several hours in the crusher the material is reduced to a powder whose particles are less than 5 microns in diameter: this powder is the basic coloring material for porcelain paints. A final mixing takes place, with the addition of a certain quantity of flux; then you have the specific color, ready for use in porcelain decoration.

Warning!
Before firing porcelain colors are poisonous! This means you must keep them out of the reach of children and not suck your brush to smooth down the bristles. After firing they meet European food safety standards, as long as the firing has taken place at a minimum temperature of 850° c (1560° F). The same goes for the cadmium colors.

In the dishwasher

I can state from personal experience that the porcelain colors I use (including the cadmiums) show no deterioration, even after several years of washing in a dishwasher.

**Catherine Bergoin
in her studio**

BOOKS ALREADY PUBLISHED OR SOON TO APPEAR

● PAINTING ON PORCELAIN
Composition and technique
Dony Alexiev

● PORCELAIN PAINTING
Catherine Bergoin

● THE ART OF FURNITURE
DECORATION
Paule & J-Claude Roussel

● MODELING IN CLAY
Patricia Liversain

● DECORATING PORCCELAIN
Catherine Bergoin

● PORCELAIN PAINTER'S HANDBOOK
Aude Creuzé & Véronique Habègre

● ART EMBROIDERY
Liz Maidment

● AGATEWARE POTTERY MAGIC
Mireille de Reilhan

Ulisse Editions - 2 bis, place du puits de l'ermite - 75005 PARIS